WELCOME
TO THE MIGHTY WORLD OF...

MARVEL HEROES

INSIDE THIS ACTION PACKED ANNUAL...

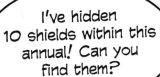
I've hidden 10 shields within this annual! Can you find them?

MW00979499

£6.99

MEET THE AVENGERS!

Whenever there is a threat too great for one Super Hero to handle alone, the Avengers Assemble! Despite the membership changing over the years, one thing never does – their ability to get the job done! Together they form the mightiest team of heroes the world has ever seen!

CAPTAIN AMERICA

Real name: Steve Rogers

Powers: The ultimate Super Hero soldier at the peak of physical conditioning, he is the tactical leader of the Avengers. Armed with a near-indestructible shield for protection or to use in attack.

IRON MAN

Real name: Tony Stark

Powers: Brilliant inventor and expert tactician. He wears a high-tech armoured battle suit with enough firepower and gadgets to level a city.

WOLVERINE

Real name: James Howlett

Powers: Superhuman healing ability. Highly skilled combatant with specialist tracking and hunting skills due to his enhanced senses.

GIANT GIRL

Real name: Janet Van Dyne

Powers: Can grow in size (up to 100 feet in height) and become proportionally stronger. With the aid of a special headset, she can control insects.

STORM

Real name: Ororo Munroe

Powers: Mutant ability to control the weather. She can generate bolts of lightning and wind power to fly at great speeds.

SPIDER-MAN

Real name: Peter Parker

Powers: Has the proportional strength and agility of a man-sized spider – plus a special 'spider' sense, which warns him of impending danger.

HULK

Real name: Bruce Banner

Powers: Limitless Superhuman strength due to it increasing with his rage. As Bruce Banner he is a timid but talented scientist.

CAPTAIN AMERICA

BLACK WIDOW

HAWKEYE

ANT-MAN

QUICKSILVER

SPIDER-MAN

BLACK PANTHER

The *battle cry* sounds, as it has *so many* times before...

AVENGERS ASSEMBLE!

...but *this time*, the *heroes* who *heed* the call are *far from familiar!*

Where are the *original Avengers?* And *why* have these *new heroes* assembled in their place?

To get *those answers*, we must *look back* to the *beginning...*

New Avengers

Marc Sumerak writer Kevin Sharpe pencils Jay Leisten inks Ulises Arreola color
Dave Sharpe letters Paul Acerios production Leonard Kirk cover artist
Nathan Cosby assistant editor Mark Paniccia editor Joe Quesada editor in chief Dan Buckley publisher

Continued on page 14...

CAP'S MISSION LOG!

"Some of the Avengers have been kidnapped! Our objective is to follow Iron Man's homing signal until we're within striking range of whoever is keeping them hostage. But enough talking already - **Avengers Assemble!**"

BLACK PANTHER
Real name: *T'Challa*
A master tactician, strategist, scientist, tracker and all-round martial artist! His stealth costume can absorb impacts and sharp objects, cloak his movements and interact with technical devices.

Add colour to the Avengers being held captive >>>>>>

MEET THE RESCUE TEAM > > > > > > > > > >

BLACK WIDOW

Real name: Natasha Romanova

A brilliant athlete with excellent fighting skills and knowledge of explosives. Her wrist bracelets shoot 30,000 volts electric charge to stun opponents.

QUICKSILVER

Real name: Pietro Django Maximoff

The ultimate speedster, he can travel faster than the speed of sound, create cyclones, dodge bullets, run up buildings and on water!

HAWKEYE

Real name: Clint Barton

An expert archer and marksmen, his range of unique arrows include flares, explosives, suction cups, electrical charges, and sonic blasts.

ANT-MAN

Real name: Dr Hank Pym

An intelligent scientist, he can shrink to half an inch small or grow 30 feet tall. A device in his helmet allows him to communicate with insects.

Hey! Don't forget your friendly neighbourhood Spidey -- I'm coming, too!

>>>>>>> AVENGERS' QUINJET

All you need to know about the best form of intergalactic transport money can buy! There's not a mission this baby can't handle!

STARK INTERNATIONAL QUINJET

POWER: 2 x 2 Pratt & Whitney J48-P-8A turbojet engines each producing 85,000 pounds of static thrust. One modified Pratt & Whitney TF33-P-7 turbojet engine producing 21,000 pounds of static thrust.

TOP SPEED: Mach 2.1

WEIGHT: 29,000 lbs

WING SPAN: 23'9"

CRAFT LENGTH: 34'8"

MAX RANGE (on one fuel load): 11,000 miles

MILES TO THE GALLON: A lot!!!

COST: Undisclosed

1. Reinforced Rudder
2. ECM Antenna
3. Rudder Control Units
4. Pratt & Whitney TF33-P-7 Afterburning Turbofan Engine
5. Engine Cooling System
6. Forward Fuel Tanks
7. Retractable Ladder Bay
8. Pilot Ejector Seat
9. Dual Control Steering Columns
10. Control Panel
11. Flight Control Systems Computer
12. Radio & Electronics Bay
13. Phased Array Radar Scanner
14. Airspeed Indicator
15. Pressure Bulkhead
16. Nose Landing Wheel
17. Passenger Area
18. Avionics Compartment
19. Forward / Vertical Thrust Exhaust
20. Vertical Thrust Deflector Ducting
21. Air Intake Ducting
22. Main Engine Turbofans
23. Temperature Probe
24. Turbojet Variable Geometry Ducting
25. Aileron Control Unit
26. Starboard Aileron
27. Starboard Landing Wheels
28. Pratt & Whitney J48-P-8A Starboard Turbojet Engines (4 in total)
29. Starboard Fuel Tanks
30. Main Engine Variable Geometry Ducting

Mission Log: AVENGERS ASSEMBLE!

...Continued from page 11

Okay...

...sending the *quinjet* in as a *decoy* while we *secretly boarded* the *bad guy's ship* via one of *Hawkeye's magnetic arrows*?

That was a *good* plan.

But did *anyone* other than *me* stop to think about *how* we're gonna get *back home*?

19

Continued on page 24...

THE COLLECTOR'S COLLECTION OF PUZZLES!

"Ha-haa! I've searched the galaxy high and low to bring you the **greatest puzzles** around! But be warned – they are so fiendishly hard they may cause your head to explode!"

MINIATURE MAZE!

Ant-Man's hungry! Can you find him a safe path through the mini maze to the biscuit crumbs?

START

FINISH

SPIDER-WHO?

Which former Avenger has Spidey been morphed with? Find out by filling in the blanks below, and then taking those letters to fill in the blank spaces at the bottom of the page.

W_ILST AT A SCI_NCE EXH_BIT, A YOUN_ PETER PARKER WAS BI_TEN B_ AN IRRADIA_ED SPIDER, W_ICH GAVE HIM AMAZING SPIDE_- LIKE ABILITIES!

T			

M		H	

		O	

HERO WHODUNIT!

Some of the Avengers have written a book, but can you guess whose written what? The clue is in the title!

KEEP ON RUNNING!

UNDER THE WEATHER!

ANGER!!! MANAGEMENT!!!

GROWING PAINS!

HOW TO WEAVE THE PERFECT WEB!

QUICKSILVER'S SPEED CHALLENGE!

With a pencil, draw a line through the track from the start to the finish as **FAST** as you can **WITHOUT** lifting your pen off the page or going over the edges.

START

FINISH

CRITICAL COUNTDOWN!

Cap's walked straight into a room full of explosives! His only chance of survival is by finding the bombs with the least amount of time and disarming them first! Can you help him?

A. 00:05:31

B. 04:21:58

C. 00:02:51

D. 10:00:16

E. 01:43:22

F. 00:00:23

AVENGERS ASSEMBLE!

There have been many former members of the Avengers, but can you find the ones listed below hidden in the word search?

- QUICKSILVER ☐
- WASP ☐
- SUB-MARINER ☐
- ANT-MAN ☐
- SANDMAN ☐
- THING ☐
- IRON MAN ☐
- HULK ☐
- THOR ☐
- MOONDRAGON ☐
- HAWKEYE ☐
- BEAST ☐

A	N	T	M	A	N	A	H	U	L	k
A	B	H	A	H	A	W	A	S	P	Q
I	E	I	A	O	P	F	W	A	U	I
S	A	N	D	M	A	N	k	U	Y	I
A	S	G	T	I	M	M	E	A	P	T
P	T	A	J	R	E	A	Y	A	M	H
I	R	O	N	M	A	N	E	N	U	O
A	S	U	B	M	A	R	I	N	E	R
T	W	S	T	J	H	E	O	P	D	M
Q	U	I	C	k	S	I	L	V	E	R
M	O	O	N	D	R	A	G	O	N	A

...Continued from page 21

HAWKEYE TEST!

"Hey, true believers! If, like me, you've an eye for detail, you'll love this challenge! All you need to do is spot the only image that is exactly the same as the big picture."

TURN TO PAGE 62 FOR THE ANSWER! 31

4 FANTASTIC PUZZLES!

The Fantastic Four have designed some cosmically complex puzzles for you to complete! See if you can finish them all!

Look Who's Talking!

The FF are battling a super villain in outer space, but their speech has become muddled. Can you match up who should be saying what?

It's clobbering time!

Hmmm, I notice you're using the new Ultra38Z-G Nebular Ray Gun. Would you recommend it?

What's the matter — can't you handle the heat?

You won't see me coming!

Heavy Weights!

The Thing has invited his friends, Hulk and Iron Man, over for a weight lifting contest. But who is the strongest? Find out by adding up the weights for each hero!

 =1 tonne

 =1 tonne =2 tonnes

 =2 tonnes

 =3 tonnes

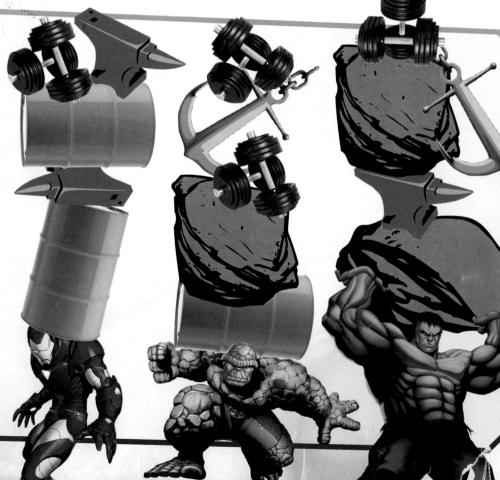

Picture Imperfect!

Oh no! The Fantastic Four's favourite family portrait has been altered by cosmic radiation! Can you spot the eight changes to the original?

ORIGINAL

Name And Shame!

Find the names of the heroes below hidden in the grid, and then the remaining letters will reveal who the Fantastic Four's all-time archrival is!

Reed Richards

Sue Richards

Johnny Storm

Ben Grimm

Captain Marvel

```
R E E D R I C H A R D S D
O B E N G R I M M C T O R
J O H N N Y S T O R M D O
C A P T A I N M A R V E L
O M S U E R I C H A R D S
```

☐ ☐ ☐ ☐ ☐ ☐ ☐ ☐ ☐ ☐ ☐ ☐

FANTASTIC FOUR!

They are the Earth's first family of Super Heroes! Introducing Reed, Sue, Johnny and Ben - better known as...

THE

Whilst at university, Reed Richards designed a spacecraft capable of interstellar travel! Together with his best friend, Ben Grimm, girlfriend Sue Storm, and her brother Johnny, the four explorers headed for space in search of adventure.

However, on their first flight the spaceship was exposed to huge levels of cosmic radiation! Whilst Reed and company survived the incident, they returned home to discover they had gained extraordinary abilities...

INVISIBLE WOMAN

INTELLIGENCE ...
STRENGTH ...
SPEED ...
DURABILITY ...
POWER ATTACK ...
FIGHTING SKILLS ...

MR FANTASTIC

INTELLIGENCE ...
STRENGTH ...
SPEED ...
DURABILITY ...
POWER ATTACK ...
FIGHTING SKILLS ...

Reed Richards
Reed can transform his body into a super malleable state, allowing him to stretch, compress, expand and reform his body at will.

Susan Storm
Sue can turn herself completely invisible, create unseen force fields and a special psionic field to defend herself.

HUMAN TORCH

Johnny Storm

Johnny can cover his body in flames, fly at supersonic speeds and launch great fireball attacks through the air.

INTELLIGENCE ...		
STRENGTH ...		
SPEED ...		
DURABILITY ...		
POWER ATTACK ...		
FIGHTING SKILLS ...		

THE THING

Ben Grimm

Covered in a thick rock-like material, Ben's strength, stamina and durability have all been increased to Superhuman levels.

INTELLIGENCE ...		
STRENGTH ...		
SPEED ...		
DURABILITY ...		
POWER ATTACK ...		
FIGHTING SKILLS ...		

Who they're helping...

CAPTAIN MARVEL

INTELLIGENCE ...		
STRENGTH ...		
SPEED ...		
DURABILITY ...		
POWER ATTACK ...		
FIGHTING SKILLS ...		

Marvel has the ability to convert solar energy into a number of uses, including increasing his strength, producing powerful energy blasts and allowing him to fly through space.

Who they're up against...

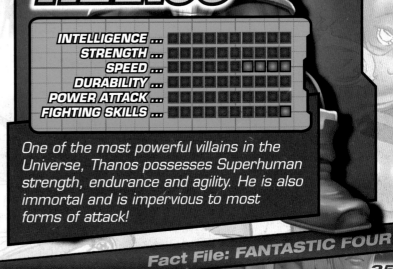

THANOS

INTELLIGENCE ...		
STRENGTH ...		
SPEED ...		
DURABILITY ...		
POWER ATTACK ...		
FIGHTING SKILLS ...		

One of the most powerful villains in the Universe, Thanos possesses Superhuman strength, endurance and agility. He is also immortal and is impervious to most forms of attack!

36

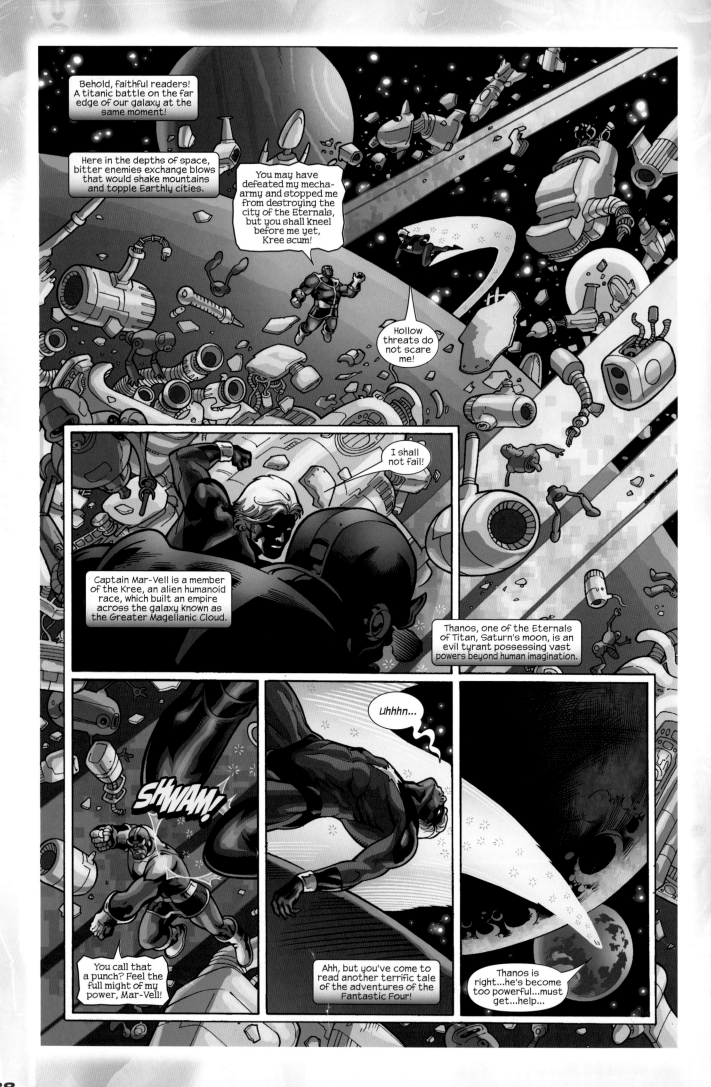

Sue, *honey...* you look angr--

Take care of the other guy!

It's time to squash this guy's massive ego.

Looks like tall, gray and ugly made Suzie mad!

Not a smart move.

Ben, get ready!

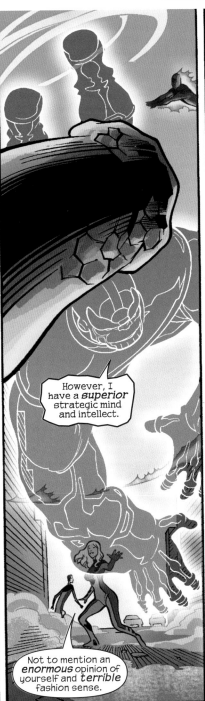

Continued on page 49...

MIGHTY MARVEL COLOURING!

.Continued from page 47

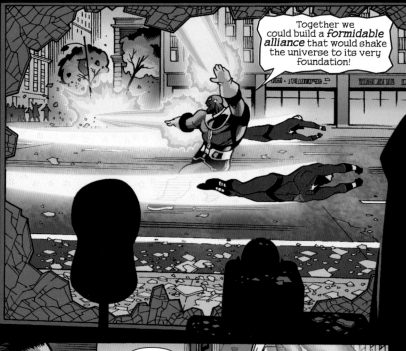

ACCESS ALL AREAS

THE BAXTER BUILDING

You'd think sharing a building with the World's most popular family of Super Heroes would be awesome, but this isn't always the case... whether it's Reed's dangerous cosmic experiments, The Thing falling through the floors, constant explosions, oh, and the occasional super villain attacking the building – the other tenants can never expect a dull day!

The Baxter Building is a 35-story skyscraper located on 42nd Street and Madison Avenue in Manhattan. The Leyland Baxter Paper Company originally built the building in 1949.

When the Fantastic Four decided to move to NYC, Reed found the vacated top five floors of the Baxter Building perfect for their needs. He purchased that section of the building outright and set about transforming the space into the high-tech FF headquarters.

1 - Vehicle maintenance area access hatch
2 - Phased-array omni-directional radar system
3 - Reed's elevator exit
4 - Public access service elevators
5 - Hangar sliding access hatch
6 - Sky camera and telescope observatory dome
7 - Interstellar defence missile hatch
8 - Vehicle maintenance area
9 - Parts storage
10 - Aircraft hangar
11 - Emergency elevator
12 - De-briefing and strategic operations room
13 - Negative Zone portal watch station
14 - Radar and satellite communications room
15 - Electro-mechanical workshop
16 - Ben Grimm's reinforced weightlifting room
17 - Robotics assembly and machine shop

18 - Interstellar defence missile
19 - Physical research and development laboratories
20 - Dr Doom's time machine, contained within reinforced steel storage unit
21 - Japanese garden and meditation room
22 & 23 - Hot tub and sauna room
24 - Swimming pool and hydrotherapy room
25 - Missile launch pads
26 - Franklin Richard's playroom
27 - Gymnasium
28 - Ben Grimm's apartment with adjacent bathroom
29 - Johnny Storm's apartment with adjacent bathroom
30 - Sue and Reed Richard's apartment
31 - Missile exhaust ducks
32 - Franklin Richard's apartment
33 - Dining / living room
34 - Water services area
35 - Apartments and offices of other Baxter Building tenants
36 - Sound and heat-proof walls surrounding missile exhaust ducks
37 - Entrance lobby

ANSWERS!

Did you get all the puzzles right? Find out here!

SPIDER-WHO?

THE MIGHTY THOR

PAGE 22 — MINIATURE MAZE!

Hmmm... biscuits!

PAGE 22

HERO WHODUNIT!

KEEP ON RUNNING!	Quicksilver
UNDER THE WEATHER!	Storm
ANGER!!! MANAGEMENT!!!	Hulk
GROWING PAINS!	Giant Girl
HOW TO WEAVE THE PERFECT WEB!	Spider-Man

PAGE 23

CRITICAL COUNTDOWN!

The correct order is F, C, A, E, B, D!

`04:21:58`

AVENGERS ASSEMBLE!

PAGE 31

HAWKEYE TEST!